LENT 2004

Daily Scripture Reflections, Prayers, and Actions

Joyfully Following Jesus

MARCI ALBORGHETTI

TWENTY-THIRD PUBLICATIONS
185 WILLOW STREET • PO BOX 180 • MYSTIC, CT 06355
TEL: 1-800-321-0411 • FAX: 1-800-572-0788
E-MAIL: ttpubs@aol.com • www.twentythirdpublications.com

Introduction

Winter has always been a difficult time for me. Unless one loves short, dark days, freezing temperatures, and lots of snow and ice, the entire period between Christmas and Easter in New England, where I live, is, to put it bluntly, bleak. For those of us who have experienced sorrow, illness, and other anguishing obstacles, those long winter months can be particularly daunting.

Lent can seem that way, too, especially since it falls during winter. But just as the New England winter inexorably moves toward glorious spring, so does the introspection and even sorrow of Lent and the Triduum lead to a glorious resurrection and hope-filled ascencion. Hope triumphs over darkness.

In *Joyfully Following Jesus*, a collection of stories, prayers, and actions, I focus on the joyful, shining places we pass through and can fully experience on the lenten journey toward Easter. Each narrative is connected to that day's gospel reading, and many of the stories address the very real suffering we all experience in life. The prayers and actions are designed to help us actively experience the joy and hope of the lenten season.

Join with me now to follow Jesus with joy through the events of his life, passion, and death in full anticipation of celebrating the resurrection on Easter Sunday.

Unless otherwise noted, the Scripture passages contained herein are from the *New Revised Standard Version of the Bible*, copyright© 1989, by the Division of Christian Education of the National Council of Churches in the U.S.A. All rights reserved.

Twenty-Third Publications / A Division of Bayard
185 Willow Street / P.O. Box 180, Mystic, CT 06355
(860) 536-2611 or (800) 321-0411
www.twentythirdpublications.com

Copyright ©2004 Marci Alborghetti. Cover illustration by Casey Cyr. All rights reserved. No part of this publication may be reproduced in any manner without prior written permission of the publisher. Write to the Permissions Editor.
ISBN:1-58595-305-9
Printed in the U.S.A.

Ash Wednesday

When you give alms, do no let your left hand know what your right hand is doing.   Matthew 6:1–6, 16–18

"Never let your left hand know what your right hand is doing," chirped Sister Jacinta over and over again that Lent to our first grade class. Unfortunately we, having attained the grand old age of six, completely missed her message. We understood that we were supposed to make some sacrifice for Lent, and donating the few pennies she collected from us every week for the poor did make us feel pretty proud. Of course, that's just what she was counseling against!

As an adult, I came to understand Sister's intent, but the concept of hiding good works confused me. Wouldn't it be better to let others know what we were doing so we could serve as a model and perhaps motivate others to sacrifice and do good works? Isn't that how Jesus wanted us to spread his message? By how we live?

I studied the gospel again, and the answer became clear. Jesus does want us to lead by example, but we are to be examples of humility, not boasting like those who give with a great public show. Those gifts can only win them praise and possibly humiliate those who receive their donations. Our gifts, this Lent and always, must be given quietly for the good of others, and the glory of God.

Meditative Prayer

Lord, sometimes I want credit for the good I do. I want people to notice me, to praise me. Help me remember that gifts most pleasing to you are those given quietly and unselfishly.

Active Prayer

Consider what you plan to do as a lenten observance. Will you give up a food you love? Donate to a charity? Visit an elderly neighbor? Collect food for a soup kitchen? Whatever you do, do it quietly to demonstrate humility. And then, to spread Jesus' word, invite a family member or friend to join you in your observance.

Thursday after Ash Wednesday

The Son of Man must suffer many things, and be rejected.
Luke 9:22–25

"You people emphasize suffering too much," complained the woman, "It's everywhere in your religion, even your images. I mean, why don't your churches have more images of Jesus risen than Jesus crucified?" We were at a church book club, and the speaker was sincerely distressed. I understood. After all, there would be no Christianity if Jesus hadn't risen, so why such intense focus on his excruciating death? We spend three full days each year commemorating his agony and only an hour on Easter celebrating his resurrection, though it is his resurrection, not his suffering, that gives us hope.

But it is his suffering that gives us comfort. In memorializing Jesus' pain we acknowledge that he was human, just like us. And just like us, he was wracked by physical pain. Just like us, he was crushed by the rejection of friends and the hatred of enemies. Just like us, he felt spiritual anguish. In embracing humanity Jesus embraced suffering; in this we, mere humans, take solace. Finally, just like us, he died. And it is in what happened next that we take hope and joy.

Meditative Prayer
Lord, you traded the glory of divinity for the pain of humanity. Thank you, Jesus, for giving us a model to console us. Help me remember that anything I might suffer, you have already suffered. From that knowledge, help me draw strength.

Active Prayer
Is there suffering in your life right now? Think of an example where Jesus suffered similarly. If you are ill, remember how he was beaten by Pilate. If you've been abandoned, think of how he felt when the disciples fled. If you are plagued by emotional illness, imagine his sorrow when he was vilified and rejected. If you are dying, know that he, too, died. And rose.

Friday after Ash Wednesday

The wedding guests cannot mourn as long as the bridegroom is with them, can they?   Matthew 9:14-15

As a child I was very righteous about giving up sweets for Lent. I made sure all my classmates at St. John's School knew of my supreme sacrifice. Of course, I never mentioned that this was something Mom had taught my sister and me to do from the time we received First Communion. It wasn't even my own idea! Imagine my shock when I dutifully made my monthly visit to our elderly neighbor, Mrs. Chapman and, after bragging about my sacrifice, asked her what she'd given up for Lent. "Nothing," she replied softly.

My eyes widened. "Nothing?" I repeated, not wanting to be disrespectful.

"Instead of giving something up for Lent," she explained gently, "I try to do something helpful or kind for someone in need."

I was dumbfounded, but these days I think of Mrs. Chapman when I read this gospel in which Jesus observes that his followers cannot fast or mourn while rejoicing in his presence. Our Savior is a joyful, active Savior, and his legacy is one of generosity and kindness. Perhaps Mrs. Chapman knew that he is, indeed, with us always.

Meditative Prayer

Joyful Lord, teach me to rejoice and be generous as a reflection of your enduring presence in my life.

Active Prayer

If you customarily "give up" something for Lent, change your focus. Instead of giving up a favorite food or even a meal (and thus perhaps benefiting by losing a few extra pounds!), buy extra food and donate it to a food pantry or soup kitchen. Instead of giving up a favorite television program (and making sure everyone in the house knows of your sacrifice), contribute money to a local school or youth program in need of computer or video equipment. Do what you do without fanfare or attention to yourself.

Saturday after Ash Wednesday

He saw a publican named Levi, sitting in the tax collector's place, and he said to him, "Follow me." And leaving all things, he arose and followed him.   Luke 5: 27–32

Levi, who became Matthew, evangelist and apostle, was the most reviled of Hebrews at the moment Jesus called him. He was a tax-collector, a pawn of the Roman occupiers, more despised by his own people than the Romans themselves. Yet with all the reverent, God-fearing Jews in the vicinity, Jesus picked Levi to be not only his follower, but one of the writers who recorded his life, message, and works. Imagine the dismay of those already following Jesus. Those hard-working fisherman who bitterly resented the Roman tax and the Jewish lackeys who collected it, must have reacted with disbelief. They probably made their feelings clear, and in Matthew's presence at that! We can imagine Jesus smiling at their outrage. In short order, that outrage would subside, and Matthew would become a valued brother and apostle.

Jesus' unlikely selection of Levi should give us great hope. Jesus calls and welcomes anyone! In these early days of Lent, we may feel much as Levi did: unworthy, rejected, inadequate, traitorous to our faith, disregarded. Yet, Christ warmly beckons us, too. All we have to do is imitate Levi: get up and follow him.

Meditative Prayer
Lord, give me Levi's courage. Let me lift my face to you, rise, and follow. Lead me to become a Matthew.

Active Prayer
What holds you back from answering Jesus' call to follow him this Lent? It may be illness, character weakness, sin that you have not asked God to forgive, or anything that shames or weakens you. Envision whatever it is as an actual physical burden. Carry this thing to a quiet place where you can pray. Sit down, as Levi was sitting, and put the burden at your feet. Take a deep breath, push the burden aside, rise and raise your arms to reply, Yes, Lord, I will follow you.

First Sunday of Lent

For "Everyone who calls on the name of the Lord shall be saved."
Romans 10: 8–13

My dad has a tough time with the concept that salvation is so easily available, even to those who might not seem deserving. "Let me get this straight," he begins, annoyed, "Someone can live any kind of life, do anything they want, not bother trying to do good, and all they have to do is say Jesus is Lord, and they're all set? I just don't buy that!"

Yet in the gospel Jesus demonstrates similar singlemindedness when admonishing, "Worship and serve the Lord your God only." Still, I suspect my father is not alone in his discomfort with salvation swiftly and effortlessly obtained. But is it? I asked Marion Bond West, a renowned born-again Christian writer, who clearly subscribes to the tenet of salvation-through-declaration.

"So that's it?" I asked her, empathizing with Dad, "All you have to do is proclaim Jesus as your personal Lord and Savior, and you can be a rotten, miserable, hurtful person and still be saved?"

She paused, puzzled, before replying slowly in her lovely Southern drawl, "If you've truly named Jesus your personal Lord and Savior, you won't be a rotten, miserable, hurtful person, will you? Why, how could you be?"

Meditative Prayer

Lord Jesus, forgive me for questioning your power to utterly transform those who turn to you. Transform me, Lord; make me less judgmental and more open to your saving grace.

Active Prayer

Have you dismissed someone whom you don't consider sincere or worthy of the faith he or she professes? Perhaps you've even used the terms "hypocrite" or "slacker." Now call that person and invite him or her to Mass or to a penance service, or simply offer to pray together. You may learn as much about yourself as your new faith friend.

Monday, the First Week

"Truly I tell you, just as you did it to one of the least of these who are members of my family, you did it to me." Matthew 25:31–46

Some people seem to know the exact route to heaven; usually, they also happen to think they're on the right path. And if all that knowledge is not enough, they often know precisely who isn't on the path. But today's gospel offers one of the clearest definitions Jesus provides of how to get to heaven. Nourish the hungry and thirsty. Welcome strangers. Clothe the naked. Minister to the sick. Visit prisoners. These are the people—hungry, naked, homeless, foreign, sick, imprisoned—whom Jesus calls his family. Sadly, they also happen to be those we most wish to avoid. Poverty, hunger, illness, strange ways, and crime are all things we don't want to think about, never mind get involved with.

How do we know the stranger doesn't mean us or our country harm? How do we know the prisoner isn't dangerous? How do we know the hungry woman hasn't spent her money on liquor? "Shouldn't it be enough to take care of our own, to be decent to those who share our path?" we cry. Apparently not, if we want to join the family, whose members only Jesus can name.

Meditative Prayer

Father, help me shed the arrogance and fear that would let me ignore those who are your children. Teach me to reach out, regardless of my perceptions, to anyone who needs help.

Active Prayer

Study the list of those Jesus calls members of his family. Do you consider them members of your family? During this Lent, select someone from the list whom you would most like to avoid, and then do for that person exactly as Jesus suggests. If illness distresses you, care for someone who is ill. If prison disturbs you, visit a prisoner. If you suspect strangers, assist a foreigner. As you conquer your fears, know that you are joining Jesus' family.

Tuesday, the First Week

And forgive us our debts, as we also have forgiven our debtors.
                                                    Matthew 6:7–15

When I say the Our Father, I cheat. Into the phrase about trespasses, I sneak a word that makes me feel better. "Forgive us our trespasses," I intone, "as we should forgive those who trespass against us." See, I know I haven't forgiven as deeply and completely as I should, so I'm covering my bases. I'm hoping that God understands how pathetically human we are and gives us the benefit of the doubt. And I think God does.

But that doesn't mean we're off the hook when it comes to forgiveness. I think that's why Jesus made this part of the prayer so blatant; he wants us to know that not only must we forgive, we should have already done it! Forgiveness is part of loving God. There's simply no way around it. If it makes it any easier, consider that the very people we must forgive—those we feel have most wronged us—are probably the same ones who feel we've most wronged them! Imagine how God would smile upon a forgiveness that flows back and forth.

Meditative Prayer

Forgiving Father, it is hard to let go of my anger and hurt, and I'm not even sure I can do it. Therefore, Father, let your grace flow upon me and wash away the resentment that imprisons me.

Active Prayer

There is probably someone in your life who needs your forgiveness as much as you need theirs. You may not think so; you probably think that you've been wronged. But I can guarantee that person firmly believes that she or he is the one who's been ill-treated...by you! First, sincerely pray for God's grace to forgive. Second, understand that you need forgiveness as much as you need to forgive. Finally, pick up the phone.

Wednesday, the First Week

The queen of the South will rise at the judgment with the people of this generation and condemn them, because she came from the ends of the earth to listen to the wisdom of Solomon, and see, something greater than Solomon is here! Luke 11:29–32

"I didn't know what to do about my problem," Ruby confided, "so I just picked up my bible and read until I had an answer." We are sitting in her quaint, old-fashioned living room, and despite her eighty-odd years, her eyes are bright and certain. Ruby is a Christian who attends a mission church, and she is as well versed in foreign events as she is in running a large family farm, which she did for years. She lives thoroughly in the twenty-first century, knows all about Oprah and Dr. Phil, and is extremely well-read. And when she is plagued by a difficult problem or issue, she goes directly to Jesus for the answer.

She knows that there are experts on just about every issue and malady known to humankind. She knows she could open any journal or self-help book and find myriad methods and theories for dealing with anything. She knows she could turn on the television and find everything from expert analysis of current events to self-help programs. And when she is troubled, she turns to Jesus because "something greater is here."

Meditative Prayer
Jesus, teach me to truly listen to you. When I am hurt or confused or troubled, let me turn to you first and trust in your presence in my life.

Active Prayer
Are you facing a dilemma or problem? For now, put aside your confusion and the various ways you've considered dealing with your issue. Begin reading the New Testament with an open heart. Study Jesus' words and actions. He has an answer for you. It may not be the one you're seeking, and it may not be the easiest one. But it will be found at the Source of all life.

Thursday, the First Week

Is there anyone among you who, if your child asks for bread, will give a stone?   Matthew 7:7–12

Jake shook his head, no, when I invited him to a lenten service. "I've gotten away from church and even prayer," he said unhappily, "I know it sounds stupid, but it really bothers me when I hear the word 'Father' in church or prayer. It just doesn't give me the same good feeling it gives others. I don't want to think of God as 'Father.'" I understood. Jake's father was a bitter, mean man who'd emotionally battered his wife and children for years. Jake had no contact with him, and I could hear the anguish in his voice at the thought of considering God his father.

Indeed, it may be that many of us secretly hope God is not just like our parents...or fear that he is! Like Jake, many have had family experiences that make it difficult to trust the concept of a divine parent. But as Jesus emphasizes, God is a parent unlike any we've known. The model of unconditional love, God is the one who gives when we ask, opens when we knock, and lets us find when we seek. Our earthly parents simply cannot love in that way. Like us, they're just too human. God is divine, and we cannot imagine this Parent's capacity to love us. We can only trust!

Meditative Prayer
God, help me realize that yours is an incomprehensible love. Let me break the bonds of human expectations as I ask, knock, seek.

Active Prayer
It is natural, and probably unavoidable, to associate our human parents with our Divine Parent. If a parent has hurt us, we may fear or resent God; and even the best human parent cannot love like God loves. To move toward a better understanding of God-as-parent, make a list of everything you'd want in the perfect parent. Include the wonderful things your parents were, as well as the wonderful things they weren't. When you finish review your description of the perfect parent, and know that it only begins to describe God.

Friday, the First Week

But I say to you that if you are angry with a brother or sister, you will liable to judgment.   Matthew 5:20–26

It sometimes seems that, according to Jesus, no one has a chance! It is discouraging, especially in this first week of Lent, to think that he reads even our thoughts and feelings. We think it's a long way from anger to murder, but he suggests that simply calling someone a fool could bring condemnation. Does Jesus really mean to discourage us so?

Perhaps not. Perhaps what Jesus meant to do was to encourage us! He lived in a time when religious people followed the exact law, nothing more, nothing less. In being so precise, they often ignored the spirit of that law. Jesus wants us to do better, to be better. He knows that anger can do great damage, up to and including murder; thus, he urges us to avoid anger and forgive each other immediately. By forcing us to think about our feelings and actions, he encourages us to nip sin in the bud before it blossoms into evil. He wants our hearts to be where our heads are in terms of following the law.

Meditative Prayer

Discerning Lord, you know my nature so well; you know how prone I am to anger and frailty. Open my heart and lead me to follow the spirit as well as the letter of your law.

Active Prayer

If you're human, you're probably angry at someone right at this very minute. You may not want to admit it, even to yourself. But this Lent, Jesus calls us to do just that: to confront anger in ourselves so that we may loosen its hold on us before it leads to sin. Make a list of all the people with whom you are angry. It can include anyone from your spouse to your child, from your priest to a politician who has betrayed your ideals. Starting tomorrow, select one person from the list for each day of Lent and pray for that person. It won't be easy, but a sincere effort will bring you closer to Jesus and further from sin.

Saturday, the First Week

If you greet only your brothers and sisters, what more are you doing than others?   Matthew 5:43–48

My husband greets everyone he meets. Whether we're walking outside, shopping at the grocery store, stopping for take-out, or picking up a video, Charlie always smiles and says hello to anyone he passes. It doesn't matter to him that he doesn't know these folks; he greets them anyway. This was a bit disconcerting to me at first; I am vigilant in the protection of my privacy. Eventually I began to notice how many people perked right up at his words, answering quickly or smiling back, often in happy surprise. I realized that he was spreading a simple sort of cheer, and usually getting back as much as he gave.

But I could never understand why he continued to bother with the few who merely glared at him, or muttered and looked away. There was one man we passed daily on our walk, who, brandishing the stout walking stick he used as protection against dogs, always looked icily past us, ignoring Charlie's pleasantries. One day in exasperation, I asked Charlie, "Why do you bother with that grouch? He's never going to answer."

"Maybe not," Charlie answered good-naturedly, "but that doesn't mean I have to give up."

Meditative Prayer

Jesus, help me to remember that you embraced prostitutes, ate with sinners, held lepers in your arms. The least I can do is greet a stranger.

Active Prayer

Each day this Lent, greet someone you don't know. Don't simply select a friendly-looking stranger; seek out the person who looks upset, harassed, or just plain grumpy. Look full into the person's face and smile when you say hello—or even ask if they need help. And if you get no response, know that you've at least done more "than others."

Second Sunday of Lent

But he did not know what he was saying. Luke 9:28-36

This was an apt description of Peter. In this gospel it describes his impulsive response to witnessing Jesus' transformation. Peter's immediate, and as usual unconsidered, reaction is to tell Jesus to stay on the mountain with Moses and Elijah. Indeed, Peter eagerly suggests, not only must Jesus stay, Peter himself will set up tents for the three to remain there forever. James and John did not say one word. They didn't dare; they knew better. Not Peter. He made a career of speaking out of turn, out of place, out of impulse. Yet Jesus chose Peter to lead the fledgling church. Jesus chose Peter to utterly transform, starting with his very name! Jesus chose Peter to change from a man of shifting sands to a man of rock.

Peter's lenten journey lasted for three long years, up to and including his triple betrayal and after the resurrection, his triple profession. Finally! Our lenten journey is much shorter and less soul-shaking. Yet we can draw hope from Peter. If Peter—awkward, bumbling, presumptuous—could be transformed, then our chances to be chosen by Christ are vastly improved. All we need do is what Peter, to his everlasting credit, proved himself willing to do over and over again: surrender to Jesus.

Meditative Prayer

Jesus, please be patient with me. Despite my failings, show me my potential to be your beloved child. Make me your own, as you made Peter your own.

Active Prayer

It's hard to admit being wrong. But that's what Peter had to do again and again before he could accept Jesus' will. Perhaps you've made a mistake, something that hurt someone else and thus, hurt Christ. Admit you were wrong. Bring this honest acknowledgment to Jesus. Sincerely seek his forgiveness. Ask him to guide you in rectifying your error or sin. Open yourself to his instruction and you'll know what to do next.

Monday, the Second Week

Do not judge and you will not be judged. Luke 6:36–38

In my youth I was quite smug about my tendency to champion those with fewer advantages than myself. In middle school, I worked at a camp for retarded people instead of spending my summers at the beach with kids from my class. In high school, I hung around with the kids who teetered on the edge of trouble rather than the "in" brainy crowd (much to my mother's dismay!) In college, I'd shun the top students to sit in the back with those who were struggling to keep up, sharing my notes and whispered explanations.

Once during a college class, I made a particularly acid remark to one of the best students who'd rolled his eyes when another classmate had been slow realizing a concept. After class the professor, a man I deeply respected, commented, "I've never seen someone so tolerant." I glowed, thinking he was complimenting my defense of my more challenged peers—until he added, "The trick is to learn to also tolerate those who are intolerant."

Meditative Prayer

Lord, you did not give us permission to judge certain people and not others. Yours was a blanket instruction. Help me to remember that I am not the judge. You are.

Active Prayer

Are you a great champion of those who are poor, weak, or disadvantaged? If so, congratulations. But does your tolerance extend to everyone, or does your open-minded defense of one segment of society come at the expense of another? If, like me, you scrupulously avoid judging one group of people only to sternly examine another, spend some time this Lent examining your motives and actions. If you've dismissed, snubbed, or simply ignored someone because you've judged them, write that person note of apology. Then decide if you have the courage to send it.

Tuesday, the Second Week

The greatest among you will be your servant.   Matthew 23:1–12

My first apartment was on the third floor of a rambling Victorian house owned by a young couple. Both worked, and so, every week their cleaning lady would arrive to scour the house. Occasionally if she had time, Elvina, a thin black woman bent with years of labor, would have mercy on me and spend an hour or so tidying up my little apartment. Her kindness wasn't precisely a pretense that gave us time together, but it's fair to say we spent more time talking in those stolen hours than anything else.

The truth is she was kinder to me than any of the well-off white folks whose houses she cleaned in the neighborhood. She probably said more to me in just one of those precious hours than my neighbors did in the two years I lived on the street. She shared with me a depth of wisdom that I've not encountered since; I still use her stories in mine. Some may have considered her a servant, but I think Jesus was right: she was the greatest among us.

Meditative Prayer

Lord, in everything, teach me to strive to be a servant rather than one who is served.

Active Prayer

How many people serve you? None, you may answer immediately and indignantly! But think about it. The cashier at the grocery store. The guy who makes your pizza. The babysitter. The list is probably endless once you really think about it. Make a list of all those who've served you since the start of Lent. The next time you encounter any of them, be ready with a compliment about their "greatness." For example, tell the pizza man his crust is the "greatest." Mention to the cashier that her smile gives you the "greatest" lift. Tell the babysitter that she has the "greatest" way of getting your kids to behave. All servants are great. Tell them.

Wednesday, the Second Week

But Jesus answered, "You do not know what you are asking."
                                            Matthew 20:17–28

When I want something from God, I ask for it in no uncertain prayer terms because I do know exactly what I want. Or do I?

Might it be that Jesus answers me, "You do not know what you are asking," but I am just too intent on my prayer request to listen? When I ask for healing, do I understand what a rigorous and painful process it is to get well? When I ask Jesus to make my husband listen to me and not drive to work in bad weather do I consider how it will affect his self-esteem and sense of achievement to miss work whenever I'm worried? When I ask to be delivered from all anxiety and pain, do I comprehend how that will erode my compassion and make me less able to empathize with others? When I ask for peace of mind, do I think about whether I might become complacent and acquiescent?

Am I so sure of "what I am asking" simply because, sometimes, I don't like the answers?

Meditative Prayer

Jesus, Lord, give me the humility to ask for only one thing: the grace to trust in both your presence and your judgment.

Active Prayer

Is there something that you've been fervently asking of God? Could something negative or difficult result from your prayer being granted? For example, if you're praying for God to "fix" a relationship, have you thought about doing the hard work of continuing in that relationship? If you're praying for a new job because you hate yours, have you considered whether you will come to hate the new job because the problem is within you? After you've honestly examined "what you are asking," say a different prayer: "Lord, I trust you to bring me to the right outcome on this."

Thursday, the Second Week

And at his gate lay a poor man named Lazarus covered with sores who longed to satisfy his hunger with what fell from the rich man's table; even the dogs would come and lick his sores.   Luke 16:19–31

One summer, a visiting priest from India came to help out our pastor. He'd come from a very poor Indian parish where he was responsible for hundreds of poor families and children. Part of his mission was to raise enough money to keep his parish alive and functioning. When he read this gospel, I was certain he would use the opportunity to upbraid us for our relative wealth and self-indulgent lifestyle. But kind, gentle Father Lobo stood and looked out at us for a moment. Then, in his lilting voice, he told us, "The rich man's sin was not that he was rich. It was that for all those years, he failed to notice Lazarus starving and dying at his doorstep. His sin was that he wasn't paying attention, and so, he didn't help."

Meditative Prayer
Lord, help me to pay attention.

Active Prayer
Few of us are deliberately cruel, but many of us are inattentive. After all, it's much easier not to attend to the myriad suffering and sorrow in our world. And besides, our own pain and aggravation should be enough for us, right? Wrong. Is there something that is happening "right under your nose" that you've ignored? A neighbor who is being abused by his or her spouse? A soup kitchen that needs canned goods? A pastor who is struggling with the burden of a congregation? A child who is being bullied? Pay attention. And do something.

Friday, the Second Week

But when the tenants saw the son, they said to themselves, "This is the heir; come, let us kill him and get his inheritance."
Matthew 21:33-43, 45-46

Lent is all about preparing for Easter, but how much time do we spend with Jesus? How often do we imagine what Jesus—the man—must have felt as he prepared his followers for what was to come? Whether he used parables like today's gospel to soften the blow or whether he spoke directly to his disciples about the suffering and bloody death that awaited him, it must have been constantly on his mind.

Did the human part of him hope, however faintly, that people could be taught to change and therefore he could be spared? Can we imagine his anguish and anxiety? Can we imagine what he must have feared, as a man? Can we imagine his searing disappointment when his closest friends not only failed to empathize, but actually refused to hear him at all on the subject? Can we imagine his sense of loneliness and abandonment?

Do we have the courage to try?

Meditative Prayer

Jesus, you suffered so deeply, even before you were condemned. As I go about my lenten journey, let me comprehend your agony. Grant me the courage to face your pain.

Active Prayer

Starting today, reserve some time every Friday to imagine how Jesus must have felt as he approached his death. Go to a quiet place, sit or kneel, and allow yourself to acknowledge the agony he felt as he spoke of his impending death and saw his words fall on deaf ears. Sit by him in the desert as he trembles in anticipation of the unspeakable pain of crucifixion. Weep for him. Tremble with him. Hold his hand. And know that if you stay with him now, you will be with him when he rises.

Saturday, the Second Week

Then he became angry and refused to go in.   Luke 15:1–3, 11–32

The story of the prodigal son is about more than familial forgiveness. As with many of Jesus' lessons, this was also a "big picture" story. He was telling the pious Jews—who'd been criticizing him for ministering to sinners—that the kingdom of God was about to be blown wide open! The gates would swing in welcome for all who were worthy, not just those who considered themselves the hard-working heirs.

It's easy for some Christians today to feel a bit patronizing toward those pious Jews. After all, if we'd been there, we would have understood immediately and welcomed the newcomers. We wouldn't have been envious or protective of our tradition or hierarchies. We would have recognized that Jesus wanted his followers to be unified in their worship of God and commitment to good works. We would have never judged or condemned those Jesus chose to embrace. We would have instantly comprehended that our way may not be the only way.

Just look at us now!

Meditative Prayer

Lord, we are so quick to assume that we are in the right when it comes to the rules and regulations of religion. Teach us tolerance, acceptance, and cooperation. Teach us to love as you would have us love.

Active Prayer

Sometime during this Lent, attend a spiritual service offered by a faith community that is different from yours. Go with as open a mind as you can manage, remembering how mean and small the prodigal son's brother was. If you know someone from the community, ask if you can attend with them. Seek the presence of God in this new place, knowing that God can be found anywhere and everywhere.

Third Sunday of Lent

Those eighteen who were killed when the tower of Siloam fell on them—do you think that they were worse offenders than all the others living in Jerusalem? No, I tell you, but unless you repent, you will perish just as they did.   Luke 13:1–9

"What did I do to deserve this?" cried a friend who'd just discovered she had a recurrence of the cancer she'd battled years ago.

Nothing, Jesus answers in this gospel. Tragedies don't happen because we deserve them; catastrophes are not a punishment. But having demonstrated this, he is not about to let us off so easily. What counts is how we respond to life's tragedies and sorrows. Jesus knew his listeners wanted to distinguish themselves from the victims of the tower of Siloam by somehow "blaming" the victims; that is, they were sinners and so were punished, but such a thing couldn't happen to us.

We do the same thing. We try to protect ourselves by drawing a line between ourselves and those who suffer. "It's too bad he has cancer, but he was a smoker! What did he expect!" "What a shame she got robbed, but she hadn't installed an alarm like ours." Jesus tells us we are altogether wrong in this tendency. The correct response to tragedy—whether we hear about it or experience it—is to turn to God.

Meditative Prayer
Father, I am so afraid of suffering. Teach me to react to pain—mine or others—by drawing closer to you.

Active Prayer
Do you know someone who is suffering because of violence, poverty, grief, or illness? Have you been keeping an uneasy distance because of your own fears? Turn to God right now and pray for yourself, for forgiveness and the grace to face the sorrows and pains of life. When you've finished your prayer, reach out with a phone call, note, or visit. Become a present comfort in this person's life.

Monday, the Third Week

And there was a large crowd of tax collectors and others sitting at the table with them. Luke 4:28–29

By his day's standards, Jesus hung around with a lot of scruffy, indeed iffy, characters. And he was constantly judged for it, also by the standards of the day. Today, we frown on the Pharisees, scribes, and elders who questioned Jesus' affinity for sinners and commoners. Yet we are not so different; I recall my mother cautioning, "Birds of a feather flock together," when she'd get word about some of my companions. In some ways, we are more hypocritical than those Jewish leaders, because we claim to embrace a diversity unheard of in Jesus' time. The Jews of his day lived in a society where there were strict separations according to class, tribe, race, nation, and even occupation. We pretend to abhor such distinctions, and still we make them every day, consciously and unconsciously.

Jesus spent time with those who needed him regardless of race, class or status. Do we?

Meditative Prayer

Jesus, open my heart and mind so that I may practice the kind of diversity you preached.

Active Prayer

Lent is a strange time to throw a party, but start planning yours now. It may be a simple coffee gathering or an elaborate dinner. Your guest list is what really matters. By all means, invite friends and family if you are so inclined. Then add people of different races, religions, and philosophies. Invite those who are single and married, young and old. Invite someone wealthier than you and someone poorer than you. Invite someone who is lonely, and someone who is always surrounded by people. Invite someone who really needs an invitation. With such a diverse guest list, you won't need to invite Jesus. He'll be there.

Tuesday, the Third Week

Should you not have had mercy on your fellow slave, as I had mercy on you?   Matthew 18:32–35

Sometimes we have a hard time connecting the gospel to our own reality. Scripture can seem so obscure and unlikely, so far removed from us.

My friend Jon recently learned different, and he sheepishly told me this story. "I was worried about the appointment at the bank to discuss a mortgage. We'd found the perfect house, but we weren't at all sure we'd be able to get the mortgage. I stopped on the way to the bank to pick up my son, Robert, from soccer, but he was nowhere to be seen. I was furious. I'd specifically told him to be ready. After waiting and looking for him, I finally went to the bank, knowing it was just a few blocks away and he could safely walk there to meet me. I was late and apologized profusely to the loan officer. He was great, really gracious, as if I'd been right on time.

"Afterwards I went out to the car, and there was Robert, sitting in the passenger seat like nothing had happened. Well, I just blew. I yelled that he was irresponsible, that thanks to him, maybe we wouldn't get the house. I was raving, gesturing to beat the band, when I noticed Robert looking past me. The loan officer had paused on the way to his car, watching me scream at my kid. I was his last appointment. Then he just kind of raised his eyebrows and got in his car. If we don't get that loan, it won't be because of Robert!"

Meditative Prayer
Father, help me to see and live the relevance of Scripture every day in my life.

Active Prayer
Take this gospel a step further. Instead of simply showing mercy to someone because you've had mercy shown you, show mercy to someone who has not shown it to you. Take a kind, merciful, or forgiving action toward this person. At the very least you will surprise them; at best, you will set the gospel in motion.

Wednesday, the Third Week

Unless your righteousness exceeds that of the scribes and Pharisees, you will never enter the kingdom of heaven.   Matthew 5:19-20

When I look back upon the priests and Sisters who won my father's admiration, invariably they were the ones who worked in the gardens on the church grounds, took walks and bike rides around town, always had a friendly word, and could tell you a decent joke. He's unlikely to dwell on a particularly moving sermon or a report on the latest papal bull, but he easily recalls planting bushes with one priest, being treated to a homemade dinner by a group of young Sisters, and taking a brisk walk with a charismatic pastor. To my father, though he'd never say it, these were the righteous clerics, the models, the "real" men and women of the church.

But they only became "real" when my father—and others—gave them the chance. If we are unprepared or unwilling to treat our clerics as real, righteous men and women, then we all lose a bit of the kingdom, right here on earth.

Meditative Prayer

Father, help me to help those who've given their lives to you. Remind me that they are human, too, and deserve the chance to be righteous.

Active Prayer

Spend some time this Lent and throughout the coming year supporting the religious men and women in your community. If your parish has a school run by Sisters, volunteer in the classroom, office, cafeteria or playground. Bring the Sisters flowers or candy (or both!) as an Easter present. Offer to plant bulbs or rose bushes around the rectory. Say an encouraging word or two about the sermon or service. Invite your pastor to dinner or lunch or just out for a cup of coffee. Show them your righteousness and give them the opportunity to show you theirs.

Thursday, the Third Week

Others, to test him, kept demanding of him a sign from heaven.
                                           Luke 11:14–20

"I'm waiting for a sign from God," my friend Kathy insisted when I asked her when she was going to get help for her acute anxiety. I sighed, exasperated. What kind of sign, precisely, was she waiting for?! She couldn't sleep. She snapped at her husband and kids. She worried about everything from whether the tomatoes were ripe to the prospects of a terrorist attack. She alternated between Tylenol PM and scotch to relax. As far as I was concerned, these are all signs!

Jesus must have felt so frustrated with the Jews. What more could he do?! From the very start of his ministry, everything he did was a sign from heaven. He drove out unclean spirits (and was doing so when the leaders were badgering him for a sign), he cured the sick, made the blind see and the deaf hear and the mute speak; he made water into wine and fed thousands from one basket of bread and fish. He even raised the dead!

His signs in our lives are no less evident; all we need do is open our eyes.

Meditative Prayer
Lord, teach me to rely on your presence in my life and in the world instead of superstition.

Active Prayer
Are you waiting for a sign from God about a particular issue? Go to a quiet place and relax. Ask Jesus to give you the peace and clarity to recognize the signs that undoubtedly already exist for you. For example, if you're waiting for a sign to confront a broken relationship, acknowledge that your anger, sorrow, or even resentment are signs. If you're waiting for a sign to make an appointment with doctor, realize that pain, anxiety, depression and a sense of dis-ease are signs. When you've recognized and listed these very real signs, act on them in full confidence that God is waiting to heal you.

Friday, the Third Week

When Jesus saw that he answered wisely, he said to him, "You are not far from the kingdom of God."   Mark 12:32–34

The preacher on the late night religious network was an average looking, middle-aged man in jeans and a plaid shirt. He was, by any measure, average-looking. But his message was not. "It's all right to have doubts about God and your faith. Don't you think that the God who made us with questing intellects understands that we have questions and doubts? In fact, doubt can lead us to seek God, to draw closer to Jesus."

Today's gospel also seems unremarkable. Yet the message here, just like the televangelist's, is wondrous dynamite! The scribe whom Jesus praises had come to him moments before as a doubter. After posing a question meant to trap Jesus, he was so converted by Jesus's answer that he fervently echoed it. His enthusiasm, in turn, impressed Jesus enough to earn this unusual blessing. As we struggle through the depths of Lent, our doubts can also lead us to a deeper understanding and a greater conversion. But first we must bring them to Jesus.

Meditative Prayer

Jesus, my doubts sometimes paralyze me. Help me to face them and seek the answers in your word and your life.

Active Prayer

Doubting is neither evil nor weak. Doubt can motivate us to seek a greater understanding of God, and thus, strengthen our comprehension and faith. This Lent, start to educate yourself about God so as to better address your doubts or gaps in faith. Your program can be as simple as regularly reading Scripture, or it can be more rigorous: you could sign up for a Bible course, an adult education program, a spirituality discussion group, or even a retreat. By seeking a greater understanding of Jesus, you—like the scribe—use doubt to the glory of God.

Saturday, the Third Week

God be merciful to me, a sinner! Luke 18:10–13

Every Lent I go dutifully to confession. On my way to church, I rehearse the laundry list of my sins, vaguely uncomfortable that they're pretty much the same ones I recited last year. But I always put aside these uneasy stirrings and march righteously into the confessional to proudly deliver my lines. This year, the priest apparently agreed with me. "You sound like everyone else," he practically yawned. My eyes, carefully concealed by the screen, flew open as he continued, "Have you given any thought to the root of your sins? Have you thought about how to change? Are you seeking God's mercy or fulfilling an obligation?"

Yikes! He certainly had my attention. It turned out to be the best confession I ever made. For my penance, he simply directed me to sit in church for awhile and think. As I look back on it, once I'd retreated to my little corner of the darkened church, the entire experience amounted to one sincere cry: God be merciful to me, a sinner! Truly, there is no other confession.

Meditative Prayer
Lord, you know my sins and failings without my righteous list. Teach me to seek your mercy and forgiveness in true humility.

Active Prayer
Go to confession. Tell your confessor that you've studied this gospel and that you've come in sorrow for your failings and to make a humble plea for God's mercy. You may or may not list your sins. Regardless, keep your focus on your faith in God's willingness to show mercy to one who is sincerely sorry.

Fourth Sunday of Lent

Father, give me the share of the property that will belong to me.
Luke 15:1–3, 11–32

I know a family whose siblings were torn apart by who got what when their father died. There is particular tension between the two eldest brothers, one of whom was rewarded for a lifetime of service to his parents. Needless to say, his brother was not happy, and it continues to divide them to this day, some twenty years later. Holidays and family get-togethers are marred by snide comments and defensive responses. Life has never been the same for these once close brothers.

Sadly, theirs is not an unusual problem. Such situations are not as much about greed as about hurt feelings and a yearning for parental acceptance. Most parents, being human, simply can't treat every child the same; and often the love shown one (and the lack of love shown another) can be reflected through inheritance decisions. Not so with God! Our divine parent does, indeed, treat us the same: with love, mercy and forever open arms. And the best thing? We can all share equally in the inheritance!

Meditative Prayer

Beloved Father, you play no favorites. Help me, therefore, to turn to you in hope and confidence, knowing I am valuable in your all-seeing eyes.

Active Prayer

Does someone in your family need your forgiveness? Do you need the forgiveness of a family member? Family relationships are not easily healed. Take one step toward reconciliation. Call a sibling you've fallen out with. Visit a parent from whom you are separated. Express your love and forgiveness to your child, niece, or nephew. Write a note to a distant family member. Take one action that might lead to reconciliation or a stronger bond.

Monday, the Fourth Week

Nathaniel asked him, "Where did you get to know me?" John 1:48–50

Shortly after Christmas the pastor in the small midwestern town was shocked to notice that the infant Jesus was missing from the crèche in front of the church. Hurriedly donning his coat and muffler, he rushed outside. Sure enough, the baby was gone with nothing but a few small footprints in the snow leading away from the crèche. He tracked the footsteps with his eyes to a recently shoveled sidewalk. Not far along the path was a small boy, bundled into a puffy orange anorak, pulling what appeared to be a brand new red wagon. In the wagon was the statue of the infant Jesus. Outrage replaced by curiosity, the pastor approached the child. "Son," he asked, "What are you doing with the baby Jesus?"

The boy, who was about seven years old and not a member of the congregation, gazed at the pastor innocently and answered, "Well, sir, I prayed and prayed to get this wagon for Christmas, and I promised Jesus that if I got it, I'd take him for a ride."

Meditative Prayer
Jesus, I sometimes can't imagine how you could know and love me. My life seems too complicated, my church ties too weak, my failings too severe. Teach me, like Nathaniel, to accept your personal knowledge and love of me with the ease of a trusting child.

Active Prayer
Spend some time with Jesus today. See and feel and understand that he is at your side as you take a walk, bike ride, or drive. Invite him to come grocery shopping, browse through a bookstore, go cross-country skiing or visit the beach with you. Hold his hand. Tuck your arm into his. Share your thoughts and worries with him, confident that he already knows.

Tuesday, the Fourth Week

Now the man who had been healed did not know who it was for Jesus had disappeared. John 5:1–3, 5–16

I am obsessed with healing. Over six years ago I was diagnosed with early stage malignant melanoma. Two spots were successfully removed. When a cancer of the same type was found last year, along with the beginning of another melanoma, they were also both successfully removed. I know all the good words. Benign. Clean margins. Receding scars. Contained. I have a brilliant doctor/surgeon who continues to remove anything suspicious and is confident he will catch any new cancers at this earliest stage.

It is easy in this process to lose sight of Jesus. With all the activity and anxiety, the wound care and medical appointments, the cutting and the stitching, he can seem to disappear. But when I'm alone with just my scars, I know very clearly who heals me. I feel so grateful. And so blessed.

Meditative Prayer

Jesus, let me remember that—no matter how hopeful or hopeless I feel, no matter how complex my treatment, no matter how intense my anxiety, no matter how difficult it may be to see you in the fear and chaos engulfing me, you are the one who heals!

Active Prayer

Everyone needs healing, in small ways and in large ways, spiritually, emotionally, and physically. Focus on one way in which you need to be healed. If you are not already taking steps to achieve wellness by seeking treatment or information, start now. If you are being treated, continue the process. And whether you are seeking treatment for the first time or recommitting yourself to an existing course, do so with the conscious knowledge that, ultimately, Jesus is your healer. Whatever you must endure, never lose sight of him.

Wednesday, the Fourth Week

So that all may honor the Son as they honor the Father.
John 5:17–30

As a child in church, I was always curious about why many adults would bow their heads every time Jesus was mentioned. When I finally asked, my mother looked perplexed for a moment as if the question had never occurred to her, and then she answered, "Because it's a way of honoring Jesus. My mother did it." And in those days, that last comment was the explanation for all questions of religion (including why we belong to a certain church): Because my parents did it.

Yet there was tremendous comfort and wisdom in my mother's words. Bowing at the name of Jesus was a simple, gentle, and for a young child, delightfully secret way of expressing love and respect for Jesus. I've recently moved to a new city, and the first time I tentatively went to Mass at St. James, the seemingly quiet pastor emphasized "Jesus" with hallowed enthusiasm each time he spoke the name. I knew I'd found the right place.

Meditative Prayer

Lord Jesus, teach me that every time I honor you, I honor the Father and the Holy Spirit, and in the process, grow closer to you all and you One.

Active Prayer

Starting this Lent signify your respect and love for Jesus by a small reverent action whenever you hear or utter his name. Such an action can include bowing your head, clasping your hands, bending at the waist, genuflecting, closing your eyes, changing the tone of your voice to one of reverence and praise, or touching your heart. You may decide on another action, something personal to you. Don't worry, Jesus will recognize it!

Thursday, the Fourth Week

How can you believe when you accept glory from one another and do not seek the glory that comes from the one alone who is God?　　John 5:44

Ruby, my older friend who keeps me on my spiritual toes, and I were discussing evil. We came to an interesting theory. An avid student of biblical history, Ruby sought an explanation not just for the typical Cain-and-Abel type evil, but for the more complicated situations where evil is committed by those beloved of God: Saul's fatal envy of David, David's murderous lust for Bathsheba, Moses' murder of the Egyptian, Aaron's and Miriam's betrayal of God and Moses. I was just as concerned with the evils of today: Osama bin Laden's violent hatred, virulent racism, genocide, domestic abuse.

Ruby spoke her conclusion, born of eight decades of stored wisdom, slowly, "Could it be that evil results when we cross the line from adoring and trying to serve and imitate God, to trying to be God?" Yes, I think it could. Exactly.

Meditative Prayer
All-powerful Lord, let me to strive to serve you, and thus reflect your goodness and glory.

Active Prayer
It's a fine line between trying to be good like God and trying to be God! The focus here is not so much on the action as it is the motivation. For example one person volunteering in a soup kitchen is motivated by a desire to serve and assist people who are disadvantaged and hungry. Another person volunteering at that same soup kitchen may be judging the clients, trying run the operation, and/or critiquing those who implement the program. Make a list of your "good works." Examine your heart and next to each item, write your true motivation. If you can be honest, you'll see precisely where you stand in relation to that line!

Friday, the Fourth Week

Then Jesus cried out as he was teaching in the temple, "You know me and your know where I am from." John 7:28

Actually, Jesus was saying just the opposite. He may have even been mocking the Jews who were claiming that because they knew him and his family, he could not be the Messiah, since no one would know the Messiah or where he was from. Of course, Jesus was right: they had no idea who he was or where he was from.

But Jesus' cry might well be heard as a universal call. How many of us would love to stand up in a place where we were being misunderstood or ignored and cry out, "You don't know me! I am not who you think I am!" Yet we are often as guilty of misunderstanding as we are of being misunderstood. How often do we assume we know everything there is to know about a person, and then proceed to treat that person according to our assumptions? How often might we be as wrong as the Jewish leaders were?

Meditative Prayer

Jesus, when I think I know everything, remind me of how little I truly do know. Give me the grace to ask myself how much others really know about me.

Active Prayer

My mother had a wonderful way of putting a stop to mean gossip. "You never know what happens in anyone's house once the door closes," she'd say, and an uneasy silence would fall as all present considered what they wouldn't want others to know about what happened behind the closed door in their homes. The next time you are among people who are gossiping and perhaps have even joined in, stop, consider, and repeat my mother's phrase. In the quiet that follows, give silent thanks to God for the grace to be kind.

Saturday, the Fourth Week

Our law does not judge people without first giving them a hearing to find out what they are doing, does it?   John 7:48–52

Of all Jesus' followers, Nicodemus was probably cleverest in his defense of Jesus. Nonetheless it was a desperate defense. Here, he uses the Jewish leaders' own words against them. They have just condemned Jesus because he is outside the law, when Nicodemus, bent on saving Jesus, turns their argument inside out. But it is likely that Nicodemus knew his efforts would fail. He was a worldly fellow who well understand how much his colleagues loved to judge. As much as we want to believe otherwise, the Jewish leaders were not so different from us.

How would we judge Jesus? Would we overlook his dusty clothes, filthy feet, tangled hair, unwashed hands? Would we wave and say hello when we saw him hanging out on city street corners with prostitutes and drug dealers? Would we listen reverently as he said he was the Messiah, the Son of God?

In one way perhaps we are even more hypocritical than the Jewish leaders: we have the nerve to judge them for judging him in the same way we might have!

Meditative Prayer

Jesus, help me be like your good and clever friend, Nicodemus: ready to listen, not judge.

Active Prayer

For the next twenty-four hours, decide to cease to judge. Beyond that, try to see Jesus in everyone you encounter. Instead of judging your husband a lazy slob when he drops his clothes on the floor, think of how little import Jesus put on his clothing. Instead of judging your wife when she'd rather relax than cook, remember how Jesus praised Mary for lounging at his feet while Martha endlessly bustled about. Instead of judging yourself for falling short of all your lenten goals, remember how Jesus forgave.

Fifth Sunday of Lent

Neither do I condemn you. John 8:1–11

Reading Jesus' words can seem as confusing as being trapped in a maze. In this much-beloved gospel, he not only refuses to condemn an adulteress, he does so in so public a way as to embarrass anyone who had even thought of condemning her. Yet this very same man—this disconcerting Jesus—had already said that anyone who even looks at a woman with lust is guilty of adultery and liable to judgment!

How are we supposed to figure this Lord of ours out?!

Whenever we face an election in the US, we hear the tired but true pop adage: "It's all about the economy, stupid!" Well, with Jesus, it's all about forgiveness! When we accept that Jesus is the only one who can judge, and thus, the only one who can forgive—and that he does!—our confusion evaporates and understanding Jesus becomes pretty easy. What's next is not so easy: forgiving ourselves in the confidence that he already has.

Meditative Prayer

Lord, when I try to define your capacity for forgiveness, let me not be limited by my own.

Active Prayer

Starting this Sunday, select examples from the gospel in which Jesus seems contradictory. Besides today's gospel, you might consider examples like Jesus flying in the face of Jewish law by declaring all foods acceptable and then instructing his disciples to follow every bit of Jewish law; Jesus saying that it is nearly impossible for a rich man to enter heaven and in the next breath assuring his listeners that all things are possible with God. The gospels are replete with such seemingly confusing examples. Study one each weekend in the context of Jesus' forgiveness, and feel your confusion dissipate.

Monday, the Fifth Week

I am the light of the world. Whoever follows me will not walk in darkness but will have the light of life.   John 8:12–20

Even as a little girl, I was an accomplished worrier. My parents, unwilling to support this unfortunate tendency, refused to leave a light on in the bedroom I shared with my younger sister. While Lori slept blissfully, I kept my eyes fixed on the crack of light that spilled under our door from the living room where my parents sat reading the papers or watching television. I watched that light obsessively, anxiously aware that the moment would come all too soon when my parents would go to bed themselves, extinguishing my beacon.

"I am the light of the world." Could Jesus have chosen a better, more comforting way to describe himself? Is there anything we desire, need, more than light? Doctors have even identified mental and emotional illnesses brought on or aggravated by the absence of light, as demonstrated by the number of people who become depressed in the winter and the number of suicides in light-deprived regions of the world. Jesus is the light of the world—the answer, the comfort, the healing, the hope—of the world.

Meditative Prayer
Jesus, shine on me!

Active Prayer
Welcome the coming of Easter! Dispel the darkness! Every night this week light a candle at sunset—or as soon as you arrive home after sunset. If you're feeling a little extravagant (and keep in mind how Jesus felt about hoarding wealth for wealth's sake!), fill your home with light. Turn on a lamp in every room. Plug in night lights. Haul the twinkling lights from Christmas back out and string them inside (for what are they, after all, if not a herald of Jesus, the light of the world)? Beckon the Light of the World into your home.

Tuesday, the Fifth Week

The one who sent me is with me; he has not left me alone for I always do what is pleasing to him.   John 8:21-30

Perhaps the most thrilling thing about John's gospel is his portrayal of the relationship between Jesus and God. Nowhere else do we glimpse the bond, the love, the intimacy between father and son. There is a mysticism, a reverence, in John that leaves us awed, and maybe a bit diminished. The continual exchange, the silent conversation, the energy between father and son can feel daunting. Can anyone, we wonder, short of the very saints themselves, achieve—or even understand—such intimacy?

Probably not, but we can try. Jesus gives us an important clue as to the nature of that relationship. The bond between father and son exists because "I always do what is pleasing to him." Do we? Can we? If the father told us we were to suffer humiliation, near starvation, cruel temptation, beatings, agony, crucifixion and death, could we accept it? Not many of us could, and yet we can strive to accept the pain and sorrow that does come into our lives. In the midst of suffering, we can try to "do what is pleasing to him."

Meditative Prayer

Father I yearn for the intimacy with you that Jesus had. Help me to imitate my brother's devotion, despite my meddlesome humanity.

Active Prayer

In the musical *Godspell*, there is a refrain in which the singer offers to put a pebble in his shoe so as to remember and share Jesus' pain and love of God. Today take a small pebble, such as the kind that often gets scuffed into our shoes, and put it in your shoe. If you wish, let the pebble symbolize a sorrow or challenge in your life. Whenever you feel the pebble during the day, accept the small pain and aggravation it causes as a gesture of solidarity with Christ and love of God.

Wednesday, the Fifth Week

Everyone who commits sin is a slave to sin.   John 8:31–42

My friend Ruby seemed unusually blue. Ruby, who inherited and ran a family farm until she grew too old to manage, had nonetheless remained in the family homestead. She was unfailingly thoughtful, kind, and upbeat; depression was an indulgence she never allowed herself. So it was unimaginable to me that Ruby was feeling sorry about a sin. She is just about the most Godly person I know. Still she felt she'd committed a wrong, and so I swallowed my protest and listened as she told me how she'd shouted at a telemarketer who been harassing her for days. Then she'd hung up on him. Now, days later, she was mortified. "Before, I wanted nothing more than for him to stop calling. Now I want him to call back so I can apologize!" she said ruefully, "This is such a burden."

Who, indeed, among us is without the burden of sin? When Jesus cautioned that sin enslaves us, he wasn't just talking about world class sinners! He was talking about all of us; the best of us.

Meditative Prayer

Jesus, I can never free myself from the slavery of sin. I am too human! Let me turn to you so that my bonds may be loosened.

Active Prayer

We cannot avoid the slavery of sin. But, like Ruby, we all want relief from the burden of sin. Admitting with humility that we are slaves to sin is an important step. Between now and Easter, go to confession. Don't talk yourself out of it by saying that the priest isn't God, and therefore you need not confess to him. The fact is that humility is a key component to reducing the hold sin has over us. Humble, sincere confession will bring the first, small stirrings of freedom.

Thursday, the Fifth Week

Very truly I tell you, whoever keeps my word will never see death.
John 8:51–59

Death. When we consider the things that fill us with dread, death is the ultimate fear. I know a wonderful therapist who leads patients to face their fears by asking, "What if?" In other words, what if your fears materialize? Where will they lead if you continue to ask "What if?" Through this process some patients come to admit that the ultimate feared outcome is death. And where do we go from there?

For those of us who reach this conclusion, there is only one place left to go. Jesus. For it is Jesus who tells us that *all* life here is passing. Lasting life, deathless life, is life lived anchored in Jesus and his words. Accepting this, surrendering to this, is no easy task. But for we who confront and struggle with the prospect of death, it is the only path that leads to freedom and real, lasting joy.

Meditative Prayer

Oh Lord, I am terrified of death, of the unknown and all it represents to me. I am terrified by the prospective loss of loved ones, of all that I know, of control. Help me make the leap of faith that will bring me into your loving arms, into a real belief that you are the only source of everlasting life.

Active Prayer

We can spend a lot of time being fearful of death. But how much time do we spend imagining the promise of life offered in Jesus' words? Jesus made many joyful references to life everlasting. He tells us that after suffering death, he will drink wine anew in the kingdom of heaven; he assures his followers that places are prepared for them in heaven; in the midst of unspeakable agony, he tells the thief crucified beside him that they will be in the kingdom together. Find ten such references and mark them in your Bible. Whenever you are consumed by fear, turn to the words of Jesus.

Friday, the Fifth Week

Then they tried to arrest him again, but he escaped from their hands.
John 10:37–39

Every year around this time, both cable and traditional networks offer a number of programs about Jesus. In the past few years, these offerings have expanded beyond the usual reverent selection of traditional, and often wonderful, films to include historical or scientific examinations of the life and times of Jesus. These can be fascinating, particularly when they combine the reverent with historically/scientifically accurate analysis. One such program focusing on "the historical Jesus," returns again and again to the dilemma of why the Jewish and Roman leaders did not imprison and/or crucify Jesus long before they did. After all, he was fomenting revolution and threatening to bring the full force of the Roman empire down upon Jerusalem. Certainly we see numerous passages like the one in today's gospel where Jesus—defenseless, weaponless, unprotected—walks away from those about to arrest him. "Why," muses one of the very rational historians who narrates the program, "did the leaders wait so long?"

Ah, well, that's where faith trumps analysis: Jesus could not be crucified until he'd accomplished his work, and that timeline was divine, not human.

Meditative Prayer
Father, Son, Spirit, let me live, move, and exist in your time, not mine or the world's.

Active Prayer
Make a list of all the things you feel pressured to accomplish. Then review that list and highlight any item that is likely to be on God's agenda for you, for example, visiting a sick relative, taking a meal to an elderly neighbor, or praying. If you honestly determine that you have no items that may be accomplished in God's time, add a few. And make those your priorities.

Saturday, the Fifth Week

This man is performing many signs. If we let him go on, everyone will believe in him. John 11:47–49

I know a priest who converted from Judaism, and this is a delight for those of us who hear him preach because he brings an extraordinary perspective to Scripture. He once pointed out that agriculture in Israel often involves mining deep into the desert regions—sometimes down a mile—to discover water. The water is then pressured to rise to the surface, but even then it can do little more than drip onto the land. Yet with this mere dripping, the seeds that have lain dormant in the desert—blown there from every region on earth—spring forth in lush beauty.

Those who crucified Jesus expected that the seeds of his teaching and his love would die with him. But death could not hold him and those seeds were blown through the ages and through the world to rest in us. All we need is spiritual water to bring them forth.

Meditative Prayer
Lord, refresh me with the nourishing water of faith so I may bring forth your harvest.

Active Prayer
Plant some seeds. If you live in a warm enough climate, you can start an outside garden of flowers, herbs, vegetables or any combination of them. If the weather is too harsh, or you are confined to indoors, plant an herb garden or start the bulbs of some beautiful flower that will soon bloom inside. Regardless of what type of seeds or bulbs you choose, carefully nurture them with water and sunlight. Then watch as they move from dormancy to fertile life. Let them become a symbol to you of what is possible in yourself.

Palm Sunday

Hosanna! Blessed is the one who comes in the name of the Lord!
Mark 11:1–10

I often wonder how Jesus felt on the day we call Palm Sunday. He well knew he was fulfilling Scripture in a way that would force the Jewish and Roman leaders to act against him. By the almost ritualized journey on the colt—prophesied by Isaiah right down to the donkey—Jesus deliberately baited the leaders and sealed his own fate. What a moment of sorrow and dread for him!

Yet never in his ministry had so many thronged to him, singing praises and pledging undying faith. What a moment of triumph and joy! The man in him who would suffer horribly in five days must have wanted to leap from the colt and run. The Christ in him must have rejoiced to see his mission achieved. But mostly, I think, he must have been unutterably sad at the fickle nature of those who worshiped him now and would crucify him in a few days—at the fickle nature of us.

Meditative Prayer
Jesus, help me in my weakness! Let me be true to you when it is joyful to do so, and when it is excruciating.

Active Prayer
The processional gospel today will recount how the crowds sang praise for Jesus on Palm Sunday and then screamed condemnation on Good Friday. Think of a way in which you betray Jesus by praising him on the one hand and then acting to deny that praise on the other. For example, if you claim to love Jesus, but then speak ill of someone less fortunate than you, that is as much a betrayal of Jesus as it is of the person you malign. During Holy Week, consciously avoid betraying Jesus by your actions toward others.

Monday of Holy Week

So the chief priests planned to put Lazarus to death as well, since it was on account of him that many of the Jews were deserting and were believing in Jesus.   John 12:9–11

Harriet Lerner, renowned psychiatrist and author of *The Dance of Anger*, uses case studies to illustrate how people become entrenched in their own position regardless of how damaging it is to them and others. Again and again, people who come to her for help insist on blaming the other people in their lives. Some patients are so determined to blame others and avoid changing themselves, they lose the opportunity to heal. So it was with the chief priests. They were so intent on blaming Jesus for disrupting their way of life and heritage, they ignored the miracle of healing standing before them! Instead of rejoicing at Lazarus, they decided to kill him for what he represented!

Before condemning the chief priests, let's consider our own hearts. How far would we go to protect our lifestyles and beliefs? Before scoffing at the idea of killing Lazarus, let's ask ourselves what every war, including the Crusades, is really about.

Meditative Prayer
Lord, help me rise above my stubborn nature and embrace the healing miracle of your way.

Active Prayer
Are you clinging to an attitude that is ultimately hurtful to you or others? Are you convinced that the poor communication in a relationship is the other person's problem? Do you alienate others by insisting on expressing your political or religious beliefs? Commit to taking one small step to change between now and Easter. Broach the subject of communication in your relationship, acknowledging that you are also at fault; keep your political or religious opinions to yourself. Remember that if the chief priests could have taken one small step toward change, they too might have been saved.

Tuesday of Holy Week

"Very truly I tell you, one of you will betray me." The disciples looked at one another, uncertain of whom he was speaking.
John 13:21–33, 36–38

One morning, just before recess in our third grade at St. John's, Sr. Teresa made the dreaded proclamation: "No one goes to recess until the child who threw that spitball comes forward." Who had done the deed? Would he or she come forward in time to save recess? Would we all be blamed for one malingerer? Much like the apostles, we looked around at each other in consternation.

And much like the apostles, we are all to blame when it comes to betraying Jesus. Certainly, Judas "did the deed," but Peter—the future first pope—denied him thrice and even John—the "one whom Jesus loved" fled with the others when the soldiers showed up in Gethsemane. Similarly we betray Jesus in seemingly small ways, but these ways are no less hurtful to Jesus. Gossiping. Ignoring someone who needs help. Judging others. Being proud. Missing a chance to be kind. Not contributing money and/or time. These are all betrayals; no point in looking around for the culprit!

Meditative Prayer

Jesus, forgive me for the times I betray or abandon you. Teach me to be true to you in every action.

Active Prayer

Identify a way in which you've betrayed Jesus. It might have been a small incident that occurred this morning, or a major event in your past. Go to a quiet place where you can pray, admit your betrayal to Jesus and ask his forgiveness. Ask him to grant you the grace to recognize your betrayals, small and large, and to be faithful. Make a donation to a charity in atonement and as a sign of your commitment to be true to Christ.

Wednesday of Holy Week

"Go into the city to a certain man, and say to him, 'The Teacher says my time is near; I will keep the Passover at your house with my disciples.'"
                                                Matthew 26:17–18

Maryann had just returned from a trip to the Holy Land, and she was still reeling. "I'd always wanted to go," she says with a new intensity, "But I'd never imagined what it would really be like: to see the places where Jesus walked and lived and taught. I never knew it would have such an impact on me."

I've often wondered about the homeowner in this gospel. If Maryann and others who experience the places of Jesus are so moved, what must it have been like for this man, in whose very home the Holy Eucharist was instituted? What must he have felt when he realized what had transpired, that Jesus had eaten his last meal in the same rooms that the man and his family used to dine and live? Was he tempted to seal off the rooms, to keep them separate as a sort of shrine? Did he spend time alone in those rooms, seeking the presence of Jesus? Whatever he felt or did, it is certain that his life was unalterably changed by the events of this Holy Week—as ours should be.

Meditative Prayer
Lord, let me put aside the practical worries of these days to feel the awe of your presence.

Active Prayer
Go to the room in your home where you eat. Study every detail, and then close your eyes and imagine Jesus there with his disciples. See yourself among them as Jesus shares the meal and institutes the Holy Eucharist. Feel the reverent awe of these moments and allow them to overwhelm you. When you are finished, place a symbol of Jesus in this room; perhaps a painting or tintype of the Last Supper, a rosary, a cross, a carved fish, or other representation of Jesus. Every time you look at it, remember.

Holy Thursday

So if I, your Lord and Teacher, have washed your feet, you also ought to wash one another's feet. John 13:12–15

I have an older friend who is disgusted with the state of the world—both the secular and religious worlds! He complains bitterly about the craven, selfish leadership in both churches and governments. He blames small-minded, self-absorbed leaders who are more intent on maintaining their own status than serving, for all the world's problems—and, for that matter, all his problems. Needless to say, he doesn't intend to wash anyone's feet!

All too often today we are so cynical and mistrusting of authority that we use our disgust as an excuse to refuse Jesus' invitation. Why bother, we reason, when our leaders are, at worst, corrupt and weak, and at best, out of touch? Yet Jesus did not instruct us to wash the collective feet of authority; he said, "wash one another's feet." We must not use our dismay with leadership—secular or clerical— to abdicate the responsibility he gave us for one another. Indeed, we need to help each other even more in times of weak or perverse government.

Meditative Prayer
Jesus, help me put aside my cynicism and distress in order to better serve.

Active Prayer
Have you responded to world and church events with an exhausted, despairing cry of "Why bother!"? If you have, here's your answer: because Jesus told us to! Look back over the past year and determine whether you've passed up any opportunity to serve because you felt weary and disgusted with the state of authority. If you have, offer now to take up that mantle and "wash one another's feet."

Good Friday

Meanwhile, standing near the cross of Jesus were his mother, his mother's sister, Mary the wife of Clopas and Mary Magdalene.   John 19:25–27

A recent movie about the life of Jesus shows his mother at the cross in a different way from the traditional depiction. Usually we see Mary's silent suffering only in her face and eyes. She is, to the last, the quiet, submissive woman who always knew that a "sword will pierce your heart." But this modern version is striking in that Mary is no staid statue-woman. When Jesus dies she cries and shrieks as the sky blackens and the rain pelts down upon his broken body. Her hair soaked and tangled, she gestures in wild grief, railing against the murder of her beloved boy. Far from the Pieta, when he is taken down and placed in her arms, she rocks him, wailing, as if she can still shelter him with her body.

I was at first stunned when I saw this scene, and then I thought: of course.

Meditative Prayer
Mary, mother, help me to share your wild and renting grief as I commemorate this day's horrifying events.

Active Prayer
Good Friday can be nothing more than a sad story for us. Even if we manage to take an hour out of our day to attend a service, we spend the rest of the time running errands, preparing for Easter, reading newspapers and generally enjoying a day off from work and school. This year, don't. Don't go shopping. Don't open the mail. Don't read the paper. Don't color Easter eggs or finish a few early touches for Easter brunch or dinner. Don't go out to eat. Don't go to the movies or watch TV. Aside from attending a Good Friday service, stay home. Be silent. Pray. Read the gospels and Isaiah. Let your life as you normally live it stop for this day—as Jesus' did.

The Easter Vigil

The women were terrified.   Luke 24:2–5

Terrified is not a word normally associated with Easter. Joyful! Thrilled! Astonished! Rejoicing! Reborn! Those are the Easter words. But terrified?

Yes. In many ways Easter can be terrifying. Just as the women who loved Jesus were terrified by the angels in the inexplicably empty tomb, we, who both love Jesus and know why the tomb was empty, are terrified by the implications. For six-and-a-half long weeks we have been preparing for this moment. But what are we meant to do now? What does it really mean to us that Jesus rose? What is expected of us?

As is often and ironically the case in life, the long, somber, and reflective periods in our life are much easier to cope with than those moments of searing joy and glaring opportunity that demand action. It is easier to contemplate our failings and sorrows than to act on our joy and hope. It is easier to remain snugly entombed by our limitations than to wrench free from the bonds and race out into the world.

The tomb is empty! We too can now leave our sad and shadowed tombs! Or we can have a nice dinner tomorrow and slowly forget the past days of waiting for this dawn's amazing, wondrous, blessed resurrection. Which will it be? What a terrifying choice! Hallelujah!